The Embroidery
of Madeira

~ The ~
Embroidery
of Madeira
by Carolyn Walker
~ & ~
Kathy Holman

UNION
SQUARE
PRESS   Union Square Press, New York

This book is dedicated to CHARLIE ROLLAND
with whom we have fallen a little bit in love

Library of Congress Cataloging in Publication Data

Walker, Carolyn.
    The Embroidery Of Madeira

    Includes Index.

    1. Embroidery—Madeira Islands. I. Holman, Kathy.
    II. Title

TT769.M33W35   1987   746.44'09469'8   86-90689

ISBN 0-941817-00-8

First edition

Table of Contents

Acknowledgments

So many people have contributed to this effort: Barbara Wheat got us off the dime and showed us what a computer can do.

The wonderful Kulla family—Peter, Edith, and Linda— through their company, Imperial Linens, and their legacy from Charlie Rolland, opened doors for us that we didn't even know existed.

Our dear friend, interpreter and driver, Abel de Andrade, showed us his Madeira and arranged our embroidery lessons.

Lisbeth Brendle, that genius with color, and the Imperial embroideresses: Regina da Freitas, Maria José Rodrigues, Maria José Pinto, Gorête dos Santos and Mario de Rosário, who through the international language of the needle, shared their embroidery techniques, and the A's to Z's of the Madeira embroidery industry.

Adelaide Maria Alves, the director of the Government School at Machico, allowed us to observe the embroidery classes that perpetuate the art.

Ann and Don Henderson, publishers of *Creative Needle* magazine, had faith in us, which gave us confidence in ourselves.

We found in Cindy Garcia the unusual combination of graphic artist and needlewoman. She painstakingly created each of our stitch and project illustrations.

Our enthusiasm for this project was matched by that of our publisher, whose creative genius, in our opinion, will set new standards in publishing.

Last but not least, our husbands—Tom and Jack—through their love and unflagging patience, support, and encouragement, gave us the freedom to write this book.

Dallas, Texas, March 1987

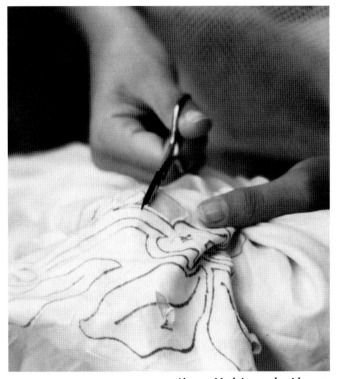

Above: *Madeira embroideress at work*
Left: A personalized dinner set typical of the old style *Richelieu*

A Brief History

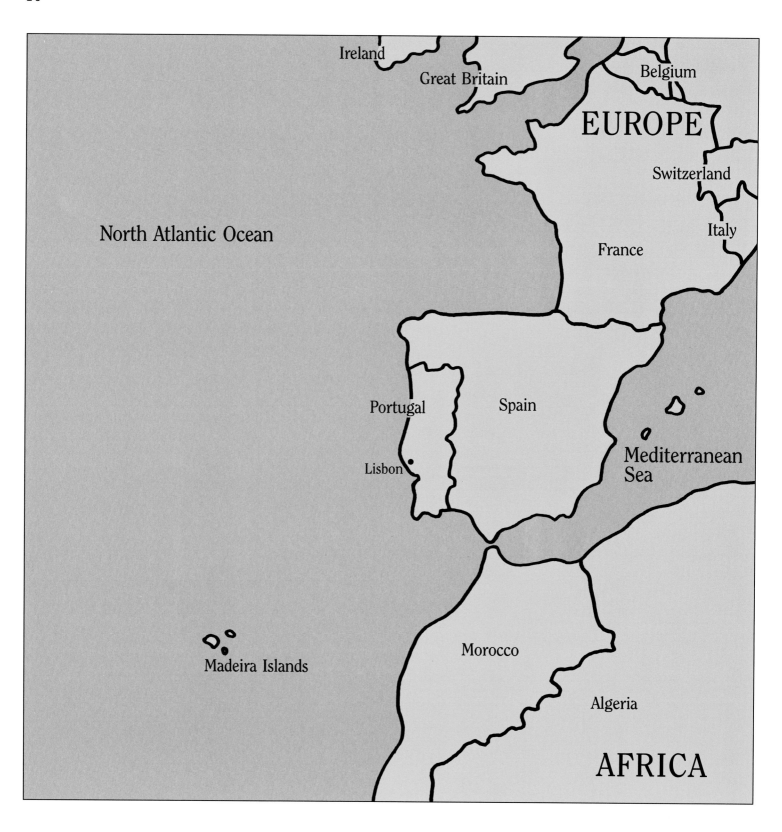

For more than one hundred years, the embroidery of Madeira has been considered to be the finest in the world. Prior to the early nineteenth century, the work consisted of the simple motifs of the native costumes of north and central Portugal, brought to the island of Madeira by the early settlers. In researching the history of Madeira embroidery, two people emerge as major influences on the industry: Miss Phelps, a now-legendary figure whose first name is unknown, and Charles L. Rolland, whose genius shaped the industry as we now know it.

Folklore has it that Miss Phelps, a British subject in frail health, arrived in Funchal, Madeira in the early 1850's to recuperate. As she was strolling about the island on her daily constitutional, she observed that the native women were skillful with a needle. Noting their interest in embroidery, she gave them instruction in the techniques of broderie anglaise, a style of embroidery that is created with white thread on white fabric. Broderie anglaise had recently superceded Ayrshire work and was very popular in Britain. The women became so adept at these new stitches that Miss Phelps recognized the possibility of a potential industry and sent to England stitched samples, which were heavily worked with eyelets and cutwork in a white or blue-white (*Appenzell*) thread on white Irish linen. The samples met with great approval, which resulted in orders for finished goods; thus, a small industry was born. The popularity of these goods and the quality of the embroidery were such that by the 1880's this style became known as broderie Madère, or Madeira work.

Madeira was a favorite watering hole for both British and German travelers. Several German entrepreneurs saw the viability of expanding the embroidery trade and subsequently broadened Miss Phelps' cottage industry to fill the needs of a worldwide market. The only creative contribution made during this expansion was the introduction of shades of ecru worked into the designs.

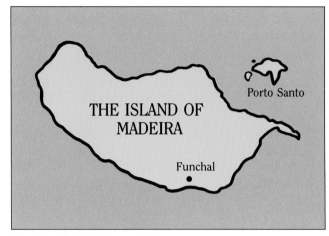

The Island of Madeira and its capital Funchal

By 1900 the industry employed thousands of workers, with the actual embroidery being done in the home, and the finishing in newly established factories.

The business continued at an even pace until the outbreak of World War I. When Portugal joined the Allies, the Germans residing on Madeira were interned and their businesses confiscated. With the embroidery industry at a standstill, local and foreign (non-German) firms saw an opportunity to enter an already established market. Of particular note was the influx of Syrians, who began to dominate the trade.

A young Charlie Rolland

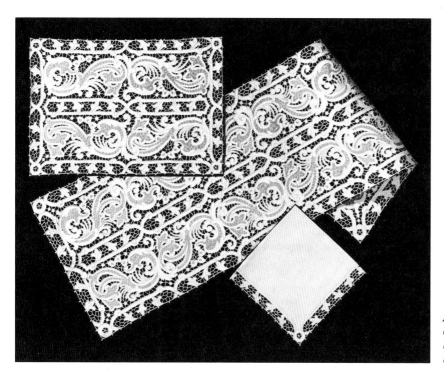

An elaborate cutwork table set, often referred to as Madeira "lace" because of the open effect created by the bars

The Syrians, recognizing a profitable venture when they saw one, decided to manufacture in large volume and flood the world market. Their efforts were concentrated on pillowcases made for export. To achieve this end, they paid a less-than-living wage and used inferior materials. The workmanship was still beautiful, but the embroidery designs had not changed since the time of Miss Phelps. This plethora of pillowcases discredited the good name of Madeira work worldwide, causing a decline of the Madeira trade during the period from 1916 to 1925.

One American firm, Campbell, Metzger, & Jacobson, continuing to manufacture embroidered lines in Madeira throughout World War I, had sent Leo Behrens to Funchal as the manager of their Madeira operations. Charles L. Rolland, who had started with the firm in New York at age 16 sweeping floors, had advanced in the company and was sent to Madeira after the war to assist Mr. Behrens. In 1925, much to the distress of the two men, the company decided to liquidate their holdings. Leo and Charlie loved the embroidery industry and wanted it to continue. They decided to form their own firm, Imperial Linens; Leo had the business acumen and contacts, Charlie had a dream. As the symbol of their new company, they chose the golden crown, to represent the crowning achievement of the needleworker's art.

Charlie Rolland attributed the decline of the embroidery industry to styling rather than craftsmanship, and with this in mind, he began his odyssey to the capitals of Europe. In his quest for new techniques to combine and create a new Madeira embroidery form, he traveled to France, Switzerland, Italy, and Spain. From France, he brought back colored threads and appliqué; from Switzerland, organdy; from Italy, shadow work; and from Spain, cutwork. With the colors of his beloved Madeira spinning in his head, Charlie adopted these techniques as his own and gave them back to the world in the form we know today as Madeira embroidery.

Charlie surveying his domain

Charlie's sources of design were myriad; the local flowers, such as the hydrangea, hibiscus, anthurium, and poinsettia were translated into decorative linens of incredible delicacy, awash with all of the tints and shades of the color spectrum. Fine Irish linen was appliquéd to fragile organdy in scallops, shells and plumes to create place mats, banquet cloths and napkins, runners and doilies that quickly found their way to the royal houses of Europe and the capitals of the world.

Charlie's dream took form; the business was started, and his ideas became a reality. He and Leo, being bachelors, consolidated households and together purchased a charming residence—complete with servants and cook—overlooking the Bay of Funchal. Charlie threw himself into the Madeiran way of life and became quite the dashing man-about-town. Mounted on horseback, he proceeded to explore the Madeira he now called his own. He was inspired by nature and was interested enough in the marine life to fund the local aquarium.

Above: *Charles L. Rolland*
Right: *An example of the old style **Richelieu** or cutwork*

A design typical of the collaboration between Charlie Rolland and Herman Klein

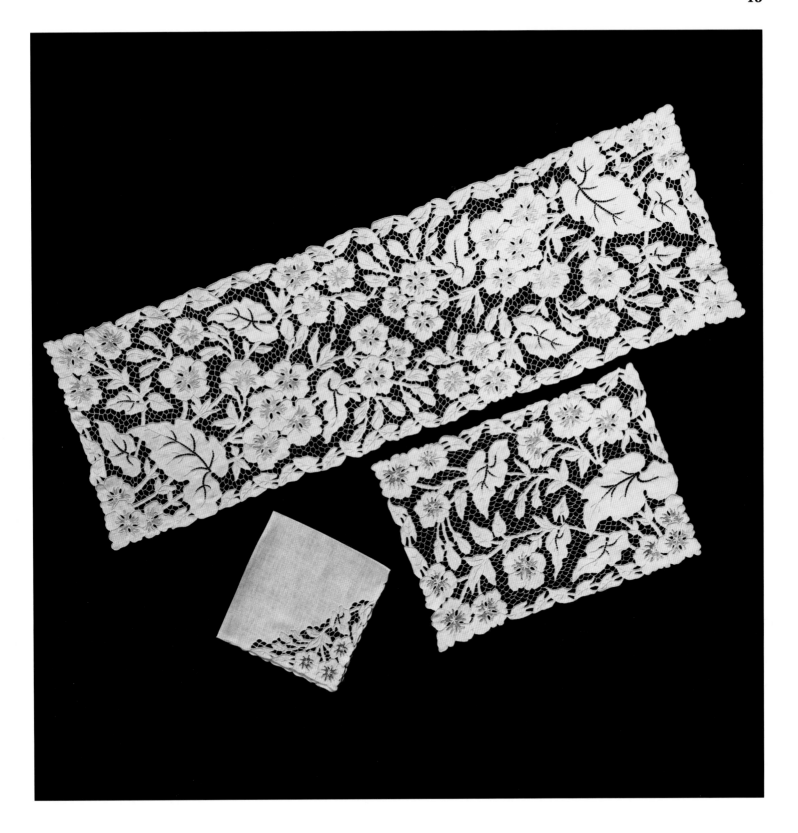

Adapted from Madame de Pompadour by François Boucher, on exhibit in the National Gallery in Edinburgh, Scotland

"A true gentleman" and "charming" were terms repeatedly used to describe Charlie. A much-sought-after guest, he took tea with the Prince of Wales and received a coveted invitation to one of G. B. Shaw's famous birthday parties. He was respected by men and adored by women. Charlie, his pipe clenched in his teeth, was a now-familiar figure in Funchal, collecting friends as he strode about his city. People were naturally drawn to him. It is not surprising that one of those people was a young, gifted German

Adapted from Le Mezzetin by Jean Antoine Watteau; originally in the Hermitage Museum in Leningrad until 1932 when it was purchased by the Metropolitan Museum of Art in New York

designer, Herman Klein, who soon came to share Charlie's dream. He was a true artist, in temperament and talent, and sketched Charlie's dreams into workable designs.

Herman was an independent spirit, a designer whose muse was usually summoned in the middle of the night. When inspired, he would let himself into his workroom, spread huge sheets of paper on the floor, and set to work. It was not an uncommon sight for the factory workers to find him still at work upon their arrival in the morning. The

Above and Right: *Adapted from the series Les Progrès de l'Amour dans la Coeur des Jeunes Filles by Jean Honoré Fragonard; they may be viewed in a room built especially for them in the Frick Museum in New York*

merest wisp of an idea would set him to working furiously. Perhaps his most important work is the famous Romance Series, designs of the Watteau school interpreted into table linens that are still produced today.

Herman was known for his flair for the dramatic and had a keen eye for fine works of art from every medium. When designing the Romance Series he was inspired by the works of eighteenth century artists, Jean Honoré Fragonard, Francois Boucher, and Jean Antoine Watteau.

These particular painters were famous for their masterpieces featuring the mistress of Louis XV, Madame de Pompadour. In these portraits, the artists captured her ageless beauty, charm and love of romance. Herman Klein used his genius to adapt these oil paintings; and with the skill of Madeiran embroideresses they were translated into elaborate table linens. The subject of each of the original paintings center around Madame de Pompadour and her notorious love affairs, most notably with King Louis XV; thus the series is appropriately called the Romance Series.

Following Pages: *This organdy banquet cloth with linen appliqués took five embroideresses two years to complete.*

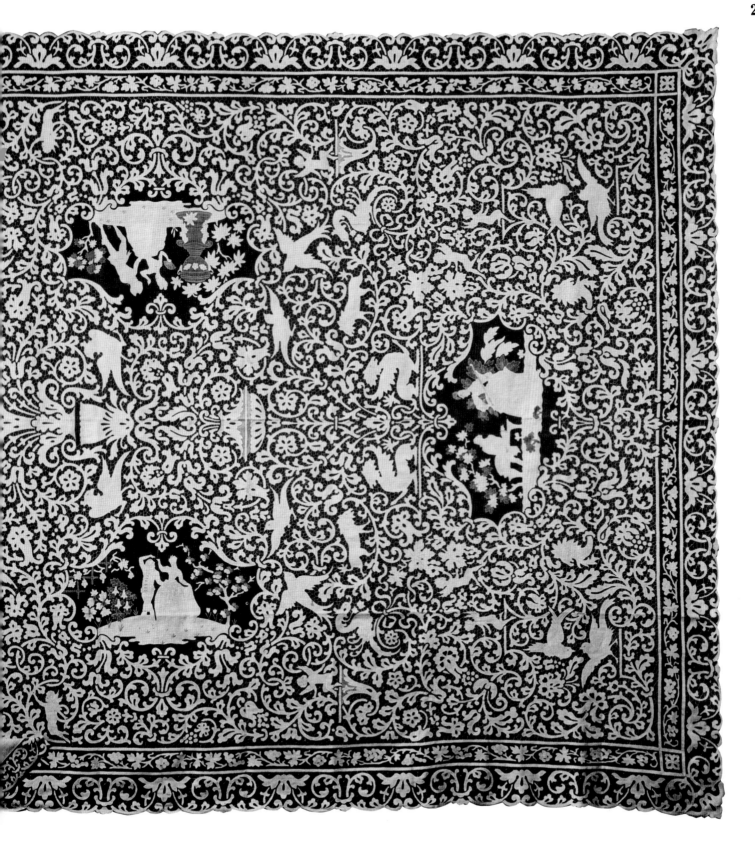

Through his innate talents, Herman Klein was able to capture the classic baroque style of the period and in their own way, these linen adaptations are as rich a treasure as the original masterpieces that inspired them.

Another of Herman's creations worthy of mention is the Princess Grace cloth, designed at the time of the marriage of Grace Kelly to Prince Rainier of Monaco. This cloth is a confection of appliqué swirls and flowers on an organdy ground, with alternating sections of organdy and linen appliqués, all in pure white as befitted a royal bride.

The triumvirate of Leo Behrens, Charlie Rolland, and Herman Klein was a formidable one. Through Imperial Linens, they effectively introduced to the world a new level of excellence in Madeira embroidery, which was often imitated but never duplicated.

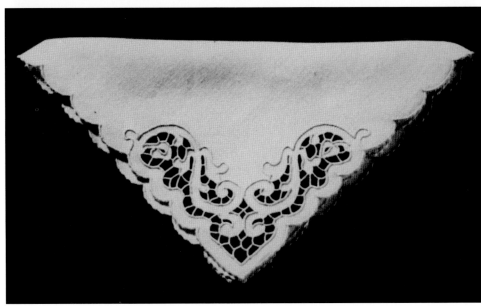

An unusual organdy and linen place mat ensemble elaborately worked in Richelieu, with caseado bastido edge

Start to Finish

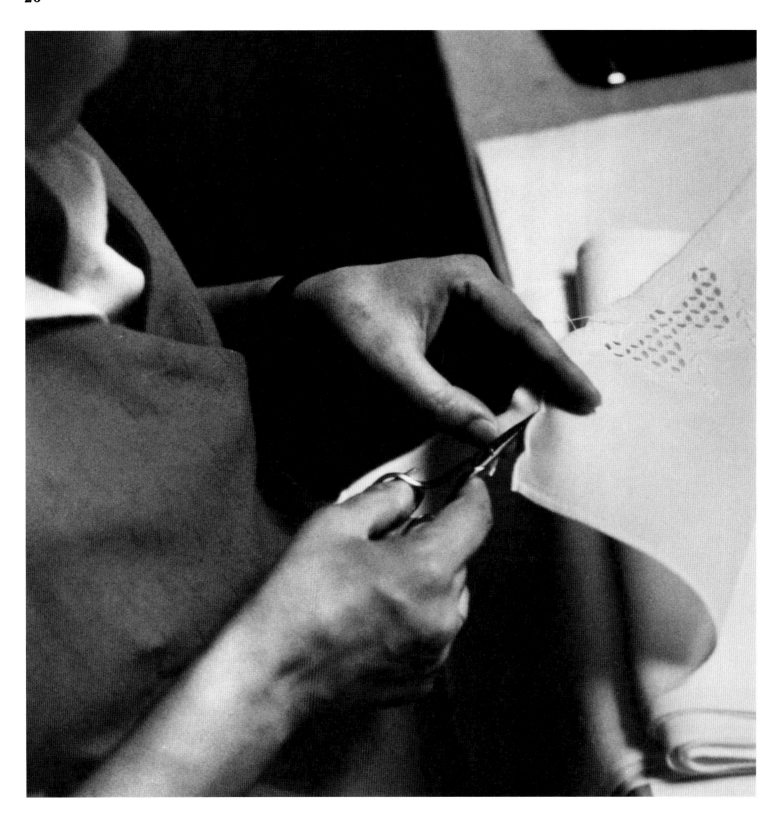

In order to understand the Madeira embroidery industry, an explanation of the Madeira Embroidery Guild (*Grémio*) is in order. In the early 1920's, the *Grémio* was formed, establishing set wages and standards. The wages were based on a stitch rate, each stitch having a different rate of pay, which also included a system of bonus points. The regulations of the *Grémio,* when sanctioned by the Ministry of Commerce, became law. All manufacturers of embroidered linens became members of the *Grémio,* as they do today. The government-controlled *Grémio* still sets the rigid standard for wages, benefits, and quality.

The stitches first taught by Miss Phelps have been handed down from mother to daughter for more than a hundred years. Even now it is not uncommon to see a tiny girl—*pequenita*—at her mother's knee, watching her embroider. While a few rural schools of domestic science have been opened by the government, such as the school at Machico, to teach young girls embroidery, the majority still learn at home. Embroidery to the women of Madeira is not a pastime. It is their life's work. It is through their skill with a needle that they will help supplement the family income. When the embroideress becomes proficient, she is registered and supplied with work by the agent in her region. It is to the advantage of the budding embroideresses to become skillful in the complicated stitches, as the pay escalates according to the difficulty of the stitch.

It takes many steps for an idea to become an embroidered reality. The design must be conceived, colors and fabrics selected and imported, stitches decided upon and counted, and a price determined for feasibility of production. The designer will draw the complete design, coloring it and indicating the techniques to be used with appropriate symbols. A draftsman then redraws the design in actual size and, with a device called a curvometer, carefully measures each line and calculates the amount of each stitch to be used. From these facts and figures, he

Above: *Never too young to learn*
Left: *Finishing touches*

determines the cost of the finished item. If the price is acceptable, the design, drawn on parchment-like paper, is then sent to the perforating department—*picotagem*—where a series of minuscule holes are punched along the outlines of the design by a treadle-driven, hand-guided needle. As many as four layers of patterns can be perforated at one time.

At this point, the design is moved to the main part of the factory, where it will be transferred to the fabric. Before the design is transferred, the fabric must be inspected for flaws, the selvages torn off, and the fabric torn to size to ensure that it is on grain.

The perforated pattern is carefully placed on the straight grain of the fabric, which has been spread out and held in place by several two-kilo weights. The design is then

Design transferred to fabric in the Imperial factory

transferred to the fabric by means of a rubbing process. The workers take a clean rag, dip it in kerosene, then coat it with a blue paste dye. This dye is then spread over the entire surface of the design. The perforations can not be seen by the naked eye, but the dye penetrates through the tiny holes to the fabric below.

The stamped fabric and its required threads, colored appliqués if called for, and possibly a hand-tinted drawing are then given to an agent for distribution to the embroideresses. Each agent has a specific day of the week to pick up new work and return finished goods.

When the embroideress receives her bundle of work, she will know exactly which stitches and techniques to use, because the symbols are stamped on the pattern. She is shown the drawing to determine color placement. From the ticket attached to the bundle, she will learn the price she will be paid for the work and the time allotted for completion.

Even though this is their livelihood, and not a pastime, the women still manage to make a social occasion of embroidery by meeting in the courtyard of one of the embroideresses. They bring their children and work on their projects together. In the case of large banquet cloths, as many as five or six embroideresses may work on it concurrently. The small children sit by their mothers' sides and separate their thread, or thread their needles. By age six or seven, the children may be allowed to stitch some of the appliqués. Often, three generations of one family are seen stitching together. They will gossip, exchange ideas, and discuss their hobby—gardening. They share plant cuttings and seeds. They sit, with needles flashing, amid a profusion of lush tropical plants and brilliantly colored flowers, recreating the beauty surrounding them.

After the embroideresses have stitched for many days, the agent returns and collects the finished work and takes it

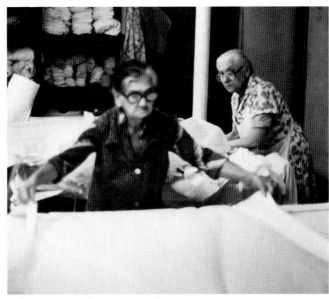

Fabric inspected and prepared by Imperial workers

to the factory. The goods are then taken to the receiving room—*recebedoria*—and are carefully inspected by the *verificadora,* or quality controller, before they are accepted. From the receiving room, the embroidered linens are taken to the factory laundresses. Working over large stone tubs with built-in washboards, the laundresses soak the linens to remove the dye and scrub them in soapy water. The linens are then completely rinsed, put through an old-fashioned hand wringer, and piled on a table to await ironing. The ironing section consists of two long padded tables with three women on each side wielding

Left: *Imperial embroideresses from the Camara de Lobos region*
Below: *Work in progress*

heavy electric irons. On large linens, the ironers work from both sides of the table on the same piece until the process is complete.

The linens now travel to the finishing department, where they are reinspected. The loose threads are trimmed, and scalloped edges cut. The linens are then processed for sale; place mats and cocktail napkins are assembled in sets, tacked to paper, and tied with ribbons. Tablecloths are paired with the appropriate number of napkins, and delicate lingerie is carefully slipped into clear plastic sleeves. Now these goods are ready for export. If they are to be sold in Portugal, they must be sent to the Madeira Embroidery Guild for reinspection, and the *Grémio* seal is attached to those pieces that meet or exceed the quality standards set. This seal attests to the quality of the raw materials and the handwork.

Only goods produced on the island of Madeira are eligible to receive the tiny metal seal with the flowing "M." The care and skill inherent in the embroideries of Madeira create the finest linens found in the world.

Left: *The **Grémio** seal*
Facing Page: *A registered Imperial embroideress, 15 years old*

Fibers and Fabrics

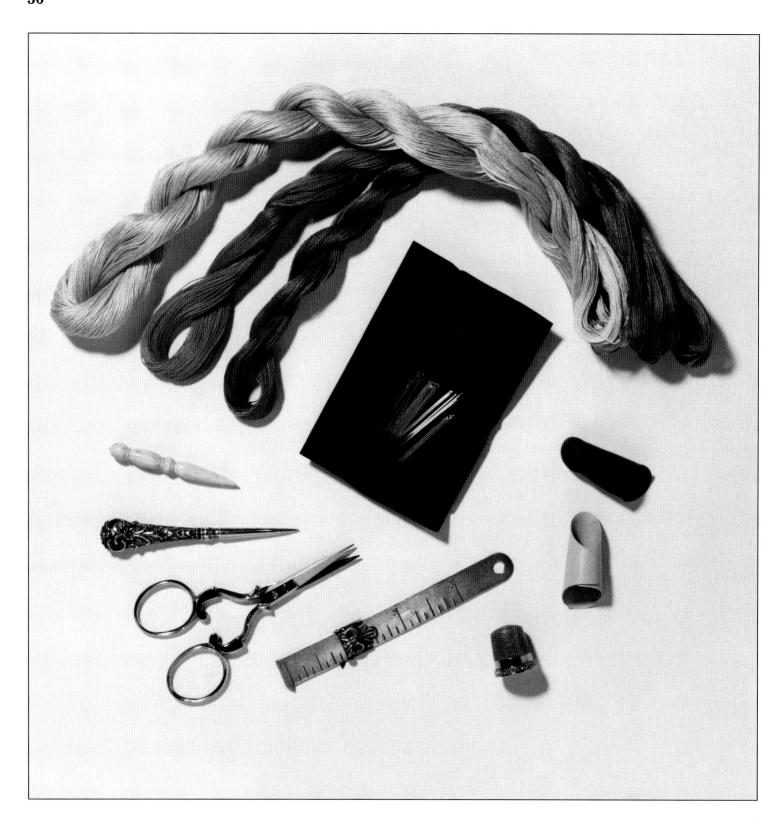

Materials Used in Madeira Embroidery

Fibers:

Floche

Stranded cotton

Broder spécial
(UK: Cotton à broder)

#80 cotton thread

Fabrics:

Batiste

Chiffon

Linen

Organdy

Embroidery Tools:

Between needles, #7

Scissors

Awl

Finger shields

Thimbles

Fibers

In order to duplicate the techniques of Madeira embroidery, it is imperative that one use the finest materials available, as do the Madeirans. This may take a bit of searching, but the results are well worth the effort.

Floche
The Everything Thread

Floche is the French word for floss. What is currently designated embroidery floss in the United States is a misnomer; it is actually stranded cotton. *Floche* is a five-ply soft-twist cotton used in every technique of Madeira embroidery. It is manufactured in a variety of sizes, but size 16 is preferred. *Floche* is dyed in a range of over 70 colors plus white and ecru.

When *floche* is used in embroidery, it has the unique quality of unfurling itself, laying smoothly against the fabric and resulting in a silken sheen. This thread is superlative used in shadow work, appliqué, cutwork, all surface embroidery stitches, petit point, and smocking.

Stranded Cotton

Stranded cotton, erroneously called floss, is a six-ply separable thread with no orderly twist. It is intended to be separated before use and should never be used "as is." In Madeira, one ply is used for shadow work when the desired color is unavailable in *floche*. Stranded cotton is never used for the closed blanket-buttonhole stitch (i.e., cutwork); however, it is an acceptable substitute for *floche* in shadow work or surface embroidery stitches, but the results are not as spectacular. This thread is best used for counted thread, canvas embroidery, and smocking.

#80 Cotton Thread

#80 cotton thread is sometimes used to attach appliqués. There is a division of opinion among Madeiran embroideresses about the use of sewing thread versus *floche* to attach appliqués. Both methods are seen, and it is a matter of personal choice.

Broder Spécial
(Art. 107)

Broder spécial is manufactured in four sizes: 12, 16, 20, and 25. Colors range from about twenty-nine for size 12 to one hundred plus for size 25. For the purposes of Madeira embroidery, only size 25 is used. It is a four-ply soft-twist cotton; however, the broder spécial twist is slightly tighter than the *floche* twist. This thread may be used for a closed blanket-buttonhole edge and is best for pulled work, ethnic embroidery, and smocking.

Fabrics

All fabrics used in Madeira embroidery are imported from the finest sources in the world: soft Swiss batiste used for blouses, lingerie, infantwear, and handkerchiefs; from France, supple chiffon, made into frothy confections in lingerie, blouses, and wispy scarves sometimes appliquéd with net. Crisp permanent-finish organdy is imported from Switzerland in a variety of softly tinted pastels to create such luxe items as place mats, banquet cloths, and very special christening gowns. Because of the fragile nature of the material, organdy tablecloths are usually finished with an appliqué or repliqué hem.

Tools

Needles

Surprisingly enough, only the #7 between needle is used by Madeiran embroideresses for all stitches. This particular needle has several advantages. It has a small round eye that allows the thread to glide through easily (needles with elongated eyes grab and fray the thread!). The between is the shortest of the needle families, facilitating the embroideresses' taking tiny nips of fabric.

Scissors

Scissors must have short sharp blades and lethal points!

Awl

An awl is a sharply pointed instrument used to form holes in fabric by separating the threads. It is most often utilized to create open eyelets.

Finger Shields and Thimbles

A finger shield is a plastic, expandable, tube-shaped covering for the finger. When placed upon the index finger of the left hand, it creates a hard, smooth surface over which the fabric must be tightly stretched and held in place by the thumb and the third finger. The thimble is placed upon the middle finger of the stitching hand, and the side of the thimble is used to push the needle through the fabric.

The Stitches

Stitch Key

Rondels	●	*Granitos*
Open Eyelet	⊙	*Ilhó Aberto*
Satin Circle	⊘	*Ilhó Fechado (Bastido)*
Open Leaf	◗	*Fôlha Aberta*
Satin Leaf	◖	*Fôlha Fechada (Bastida)*
Eyelet Edge	⊚	*Ilhó Aberto de Grega*
Shadow Work	✾	*Ponto de Sombra*
Satin Stitch	◿	*Chão*
Seed Stitch	♡	*Pesponto*
Padded Satin	✐	*Bastido*
Long and Short	✐	*Matiz*
Pulled Thread (Fil Tiré)	◌	*Arrendado*
Pin Stitch	⤳	*Ponto Francês*
Outline	∿	*Ponto de Corda*
Whipped Running Stitch	⌒	*Ponto de Cordão*
Closed Blanket-Buttonhole	⌣	*Caseado Liso*
Cutwork with Bars	⊟⊟⊟	*Richelieu*
Broderie Anglaise with Bars	⊟⊟⊟	*Oficial*
Scalloped Blanket-Buttonhole	⌣⌣⌣	*Caseado Bastido*

The stitches of Madeira embroidery presented herein are shown as they are worked by the Madeiran embroideresses. It must be remembered that these women stitch for income, and time is money. In the past 150 years, they have found the most expeditious means to an artistic end. These are not the customary embroidery methods. They are simply the methods used by the world's premier embroideresses.

The stitches are described in order from the easiest to the most difficult, as rated by the *Grémio*. The common English name is given first, followed by the stitch symbol and its Portuguese name.

Threading the small eye of the #7 needle takes a bit of practice. Trial and many errors have shown that cutting the end of the thread at an angle with the twist is helpful. Moistening the thread and then rolling it firmly between the thumb and forefinger, tightening the twist, is a must. Hold your breath and thread up. It can be done with practice—three-year-old Madeirans do it!

Except where noted, the stitches are tied in with a tiny backstitch done from the front of the work. The stitches are tied off on the back with a loop knot.

It is interesting to note that the Madeirans stitch with a very long tail, which ends about two to three inches above the fabric. Stitching with this shorter thread allows better control. Continually moving the needle up the thread prevents the thread from fraying.

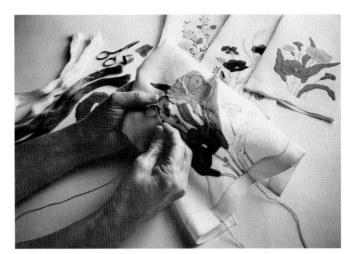

A Portuguese embroideress creating an heirloom

Rondels •

Granitos

Tie in with a tiny backstitch in the middle of the dot. Place the needle through the fabric at the top of the dot and out at the bottom, scooping the stitch with the fabric stretched tight over the finger shield. Repeat this wrap six to seven times through the same holes. Tie off on the back with a loop knot.

Granitos Bastido

If a fuller rondel, known as *bastido* (padded satin), is desired, wrap a total of ten to eleven times.

Viuva (Widow)

The *viuva* flower, as shown in the photograph at right is comprised of five *granitos bastido* petals radiating from the center. The center may be either an open eyelet or a *granitos bastido*.

Estrêla (Star Flower)

Granitos form the petals and center of the *estrêla,* as shown in the bottom photograph at right. The direction of the *granitos* is circular.

Top: *Granitos (rondel) and granitos bastido (fuller rondel) used in profusion to define and enhance the designs*
Bottom: *An Estrêla greatly enlarged*

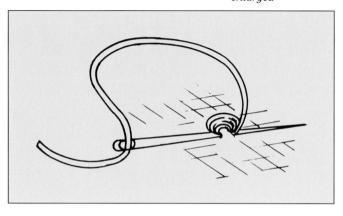

Open Eyelet ⊘

Ilhó Aberto

The open eyelet is padded in a unique manner. The thread tail is left loose on the front of the work. Start at the bottom right-hand side of the circle, take a tiny nip of fabric, and leave the tail about ½" long.

Lay the thread up the right side of the circle, take a nip of fabric, and lay the thread along the top. Repeat to form a square. At the last corner, sink the thread and come up on the outside of the drawn circle, as shown in diagram 1.

With an awl, pierce the fabric, as shown in diagram 2, enlarging the hole to the padding threads.

Take the needle down the center hole, as shown in diagram 3, and pulling tightly, come up on the outside edge. The stitches must be very close and pulled tightly to give a uniform wrap.

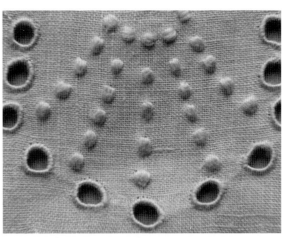

Open eyelets used in combination with **granitos**

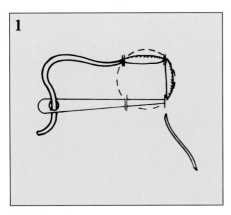

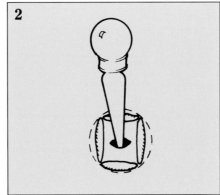

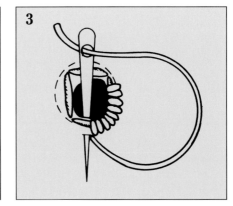

Satin Circle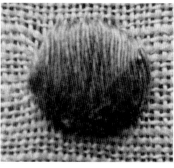

Ilhó Fechado

To begin this stitch, hold the fabric tightly stretched over the finger shield so that the direction of the finished satin stitch will be vertical. Tie in with a backstitch at the upper right-hand side of the circle and continue with a split stitch around the perimeter, as shown in diagram 1. Bring the needle up just inside the split stitch and lace the thread horizontally, picking up one thread of fabric on each side of the inside of the circle, as shown in diagram 2.

Place the first satin stitch three thread widths from the edge of the circle. Work subsequent stitches in a vertical direction, fitting them snugly side by side, as shown in diagram 3.

Place the last stitch three thread widths from the other side of the circle, take the thread to the back, and tie off with a loop knot.

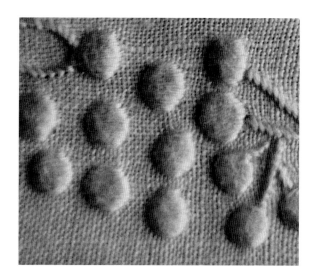

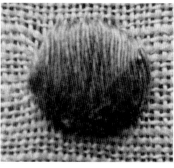

Above: *A group of satin circles forming a cluster of grapes*
Right: *Extreme close-up of a satin circle*

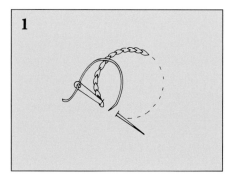

1

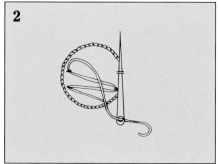

2

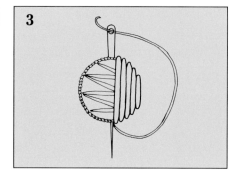

3

Open Leaf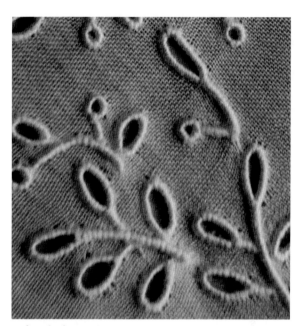
Fôlha Aberta

With the fabric stretched tightly over the finger shield, and with small, very sharp, pointed scissors, slit the middle third of the motif, as shown in diagram 1.

Take a nip of fabric, leaving a loose tail ½" from the bottom point of the motif. Take the thread to the top and down the other side, creating a V-shape, as seen in diagram 2. Take the thread to the back and come up on the outside of the drawn bottom point. Start at this point with the longest

stitch (the first three stitches will be longer than the rest), going down in the center hole and coming up on the outside edge with a wrapping motion, pulling tightly, as shown in diagram 3.

Continue in a clockwise direction around the motif. The last two stitches should be slightly elongated to match the beginning stitches. With the last stitch, go to the back under the first stitch and tie off with a loop knot.

A frond of open leaves

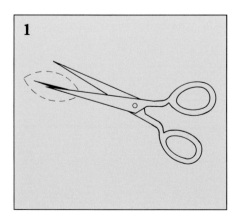

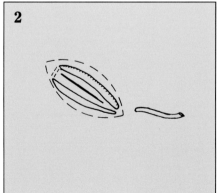

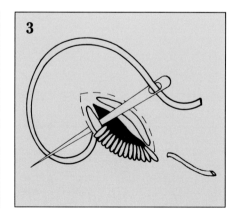

Satin Leaf

Fôlha Fechada

Fôlha fechada is prepared in a manner that allows the padding stitches to lie on the top of the fabric. This enables the work to lie flat and not buckle.

Starting on the outside third of the motif, work the padding stitches in a figure eight configuration, making each figure eight a bit larger than the previous one, as shown in diagram 1. When the entire motif is filled, check to see that the padding does not fall over the design outline. If it does, simply whip the threads together until they are inside the outline.

Bring the needle up on the outside top of the design and take a small straight stitch. Continue with satin stitches, keeping the stitches very close together, as shown in diagram 2, but not so close that they overlap. When finished, take the thread to the back of the work and tie off.

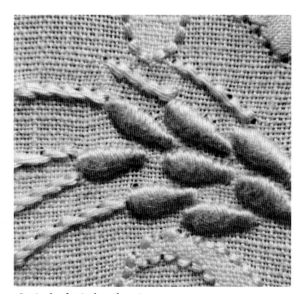

Satin leaf stitches forming a sheaf of wheat

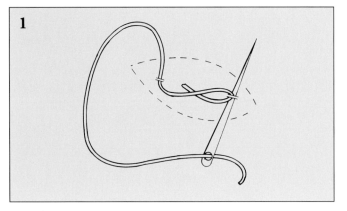

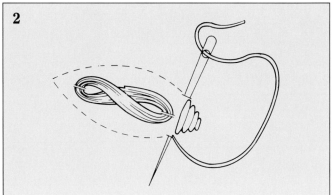

Eyelet Edge ⊘

Ilhó Aberto de Grega

The bottom half of the circles are worked in *caseado liso* (closed blanket-buttonhole, see page 62), and the tops are wrapped. Both halves must be padded in a serpentine fashion, as illustrated in diagrams 1 and 2.

Pierce the center of the circles with an awl, as shown in diagram 2, enlarging the hole to the padding configuration.

Starting at the left-hand edge, begin working the bottom half of the circles using *caseado* as shown in

diagram 3. At the end of the last circle, sink the thread and finish off the last stitch.

Flip the fabric upside down and bring the needle up one thread away from the last *caseado* stitch. Finish the remaining halves of the circles by taking the needle down in the center hole and bringing it up on the outside edge of the circle, pulling the wrap tightly, as shown in diagram 4. The wrapped edge must meet the *caseado* edge where the circles join.

A delicate eyelet border for a linen serviette

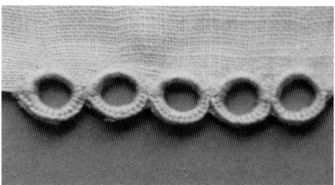

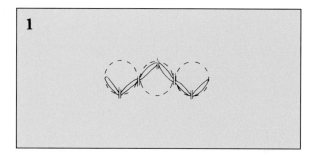

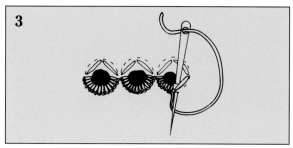

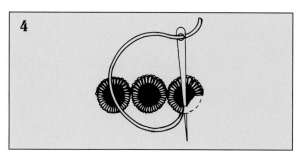

Shadow Work 💜

Ponto de Sombra

Ponto de sombra is used when a look lighter than appliqué is desired. It is usually used on sheer fabrics. *Ponto de sombra* is worked from the wrong side of the fabric with a herringbone variation, from left to right with the needle always pointing to the left.

Tie in with a backstitch at the top of the design. With the thread above the needle, take a ¹⁄₁₆" stitch over the backstitch, making sure the needle crosses over the thread, as shown in diagram 1.

Move to the lower edge of the motif and, with the thread below the needle, take a ⅛" stitch, making sure that the first and second stitches come together at the point of the motif, as seen in diagram 2.

Detail of shadow work flowers on a chiffon scarf

The next stitch is taken on the upper edge, as seen in diagram 3. Again, the thread is above the needle, and this third stitch is ⅛" long. This herringbone variation is created by having the thread above the needle on the upper stitches and below the needle on the lower stitches, as seen in diagrams 4 and 5. This variation allows the thread to lie closer to the ground fabric, producing a more intense color on the front.

If a motif divides, as in the heart-shaped diagram, work the wide area first. As the split is reached, work the upper or lower portion (decided by the last stitch taken), as seen in diagram 6. Tie in a new thread and work the remaining portion as previously described. Tie off with two backstitches hidden in the outline of the design.

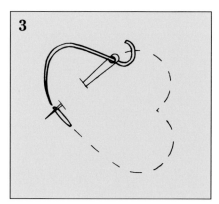

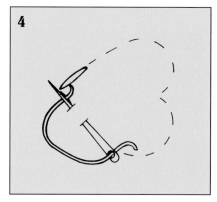

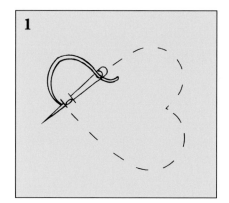

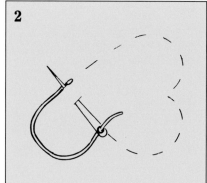

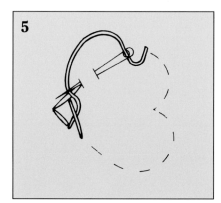

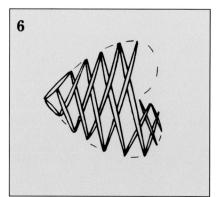

Satin Stitch

Chão

Chão is not a padded stitch. Rather, it is a series of very closely worked oblique (45° angle) long stitches.

The fabric is tightly stretched over the finger shield while stitching.

Take the first stitch one thread width inside the design area. This prevents beginning with too small a stitch and sets the angle for succeeding stitches. It also retains the shape of the motif.

Above: *Enlargement of **chão**, giving the illusion of padding due to the loft of the **floche** thread*

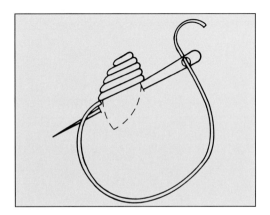

Seed Stitch ♡

Pesponto

Pesponto is a shading technique used with great effectiveness by the Madeirans. It is often seen in the heart of a flower, under the curve of a petal, or standing alone as in the seeds on a strawberry. It is used on top of appliqués and on the base fabric in cutwork. With all its effectiveness, it is a very simple stitch.

Pesponto is a series of running backstitches worked in a concentric pattern. Begin at the outside of the design shape and turn the work as the pattern progresses, as shown in diagram 1. Diagram 2 illustrates the finished seeded area.

Even when the thread and fabric are the same value, an interesting light play results, creating a subdued effect, as shown in the photograph at right. A contrasting thread emphasizes the shading.

Right: *Dimensional effect achieved with pesponto*

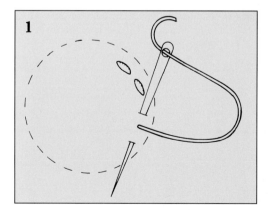

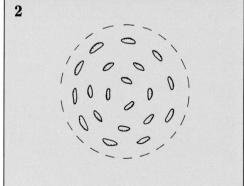

Padded Satin

Bastido

While the *Grémio* lists *bastido* as a stitch, it is in reality an effect rather than a specific stitch. It denotes heavily padded high relief. While a monogram might employ *ponto de cordão* (whipped running stitch), when it is *bastido,* more than normal padding is used. Any shape that is heavily padded is *bastido.*

The padding is worked in increasing sizes of figure eights. Begin in the middle of the motif with a small stitch, as seen in diagram 1. This type of padding enables the ground fabric to lie flat against whatever surface it may touch.

Fleur-de-lis using bastido principle

Curved bastido greatly enlarged

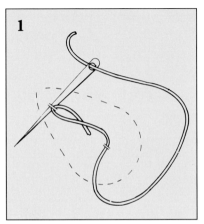

1

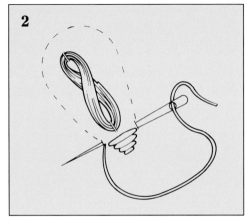

2

Long and Short

Matiz

While at first glance *matiz* resembles crewel long and short, it is actually worked a bit differently. No holes are shared. Succeeding rows encroach the stitches of the preceding row. The direction of the stitches may either follow the outline or may radiate from a central point of the motif.

On heavier fabrics, *matiz* replaces *ponto de sombra* (shadow work) and is often used with animal designs and birds to create the impression of motion.

A shaded flower worked completely in matiz

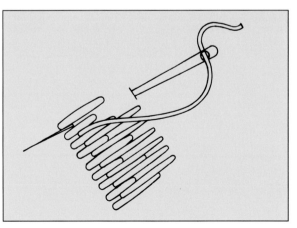

Pulled Thread (Fil Tiré)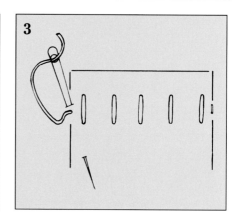

Arrendado

Arrendado is used as a filling stitch to give an open, lacy effect. It is always surrounded by another stitch, such as *ponto de cordão* (whipped running stitch, see page 61). It is worked in two steps: rows of vertical stitches followed by rows of horizontal stitches. Begin with a backstitch on the outline of the area to be filled, as shown in diagram 1. Move inside ¹⁄₁₆" and make a row of vertical stitches ¹⁄₁₆" tall and ¹⁄₁₆" apart. Pull each

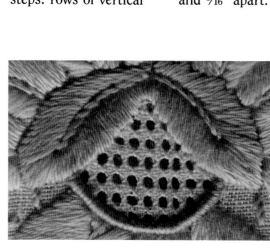

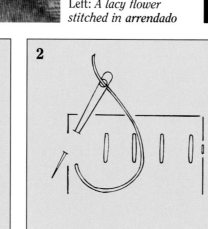

Right: *Handkerchief corner embellished with arrendado and surrounded with ponto de cordão*
Left: *A lacy flower stitched in arrendado*

1

2

3

stitch tightly making sure the last stitch comes up in the outline, as illustrated in diagram 2.

Take a backstitch and start the next row, as seen in diagram 3. Continue until the area is filled, as shown in diagrams 4 and 5, making sure that the last stitch of the last row comes up in the outline. Take a backstitch and come up under the next-to-last full stitch, as seen in diagram 6.

Rotate the work a quarter turn to the left and work another row as shown in diagram 7. Take a backstitch in the outline at the end of the row, as before. Continue until the area is filled, forming a series of squares with holes between each square.

Take long padding stitches on the outline of the area, as seen in diagram 8, and use *ponto de cordão* to frame the *arrendado,* as illustrated in diagram 9.

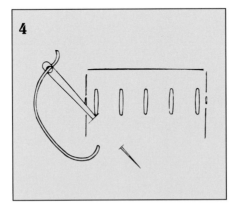

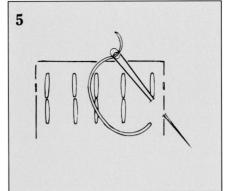

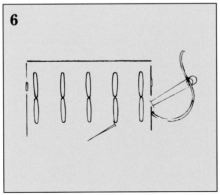

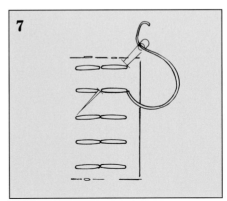

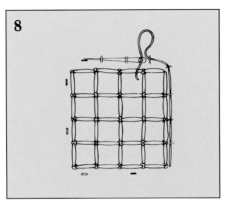

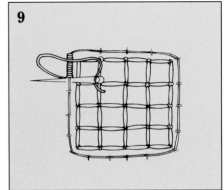

Pin Stitch

Ponto Francês

Ponto francês is one of the most-used Madeiran stitches. It is used to attach appliqués and to fasten appliqué and repliqué hems. It produces a series of holes along the line of the stitch, which gives a break between the appliqué and the ground fabric, or the illusion of tiny hemstitching along the edge. Ideally, each of the stitches should be about ¹⁄₁₆" long and pulled tightly to create holes. *Ponto francês* is worked from right to left, with the piece to be attached at the top.

Tie in with a backstitch, bringing the needle up through only one or two threads of the folded layer of the piece to be attached, as seen in diagram 1.

Bring the needle down, sharing with the previous stitch, and back up ¹⁄₁₆" to the left. Go back to the bottom of the vertical stitch, come up through one or two threads of the folded layer, and back down in the end of the horizontal stitch, sharing holes and pulling tightly as shown in diagrams, 2, 3, and 4. Diagram 5 shows the completed stitches.

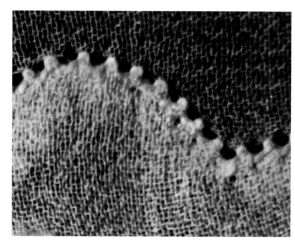

Close-up of Pin Stitch

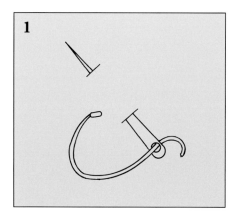

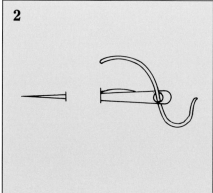

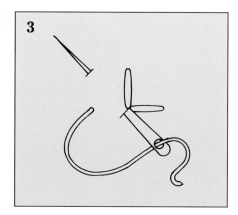

Pin-stitched appliqué using proper thread tension

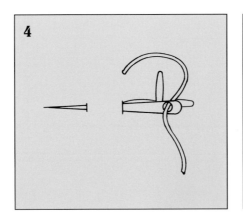

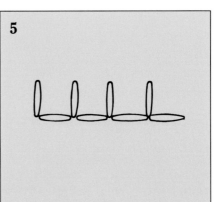

Outline

Ponto de Corda

While *ponto de corda* appears to be one of the simplest of the Madeiran stitches, it must be very carefully executed to achieve maximum effect. Small, even stitches must be taken, always sharing holes with the previously worked stitch. *Ponto de corda* is always worked with the thread below the needle as shown in diagram 1.

If a finer, flatter definition is desired, use the reverse of the outline stitch—*ponto atraz,* or backstitch. This is most often seen in the embellishment of appliqués, such as the veins in the leaves in the photograph at the right. See diagram 2 for *ponto atraz.*

Top: *Tendril formed with ponto de corda*
Bottom: *Ponto atraz worked on leaf appliqué*

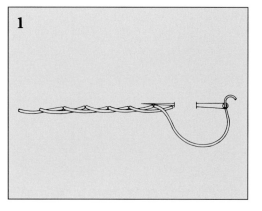

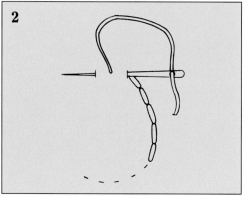

Whipped Running Stitch

Ponto de Cordão

Ponto de cordão is used when a heavy stem or line is desired. It is a whipped running stitch, with long stitches being taken for the padding. The number of rows of running stitches taken will depend upon the heaviness desired.

Lay the running stitches as shown in diagram 1. To end the padding, simply cut the thread or lay the end along the padding stitches, taking tiny nips of fabric beneath the padding. The wrapping stitches should be at a right angle to the design line, as seen in diagram 2.

The high relief effect of ponto de cordão

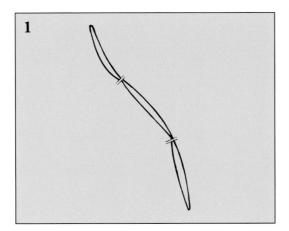

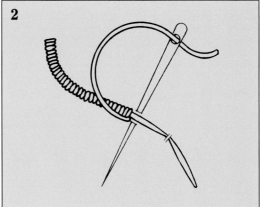

Closed Blanket-Buttonhole

Caseado Liso

Caseado liso utilizes the closed blanket-buttonhole stitch. *"Liso"* means smooth, and all *caseado liso* stitches are uniform in size. The looped edge (base) of the *caseado* is called the purl. The purl will always face the edge to be cut. The stitch must begin at the base; otherwise, a detached chain stitch will result.

The padding for *caseado liso* consists of a zigzag running stitch, as shown in diagram 1. A ¹⁄₁₆" tail is left at the top of a scallop; and the padding is run from the top to the base of the curve, catching two or three threads, and on to the peak of the next scallop. The beginning and ending tails are left loose. Do not pull these padding stitches too tightly, as the fabric will pucker.

Tie in with a backstitch at the purl edge (base) and continue as shown in diagram 2. When there are two to three inches of thread left, it's time to change to a new thread. Lay the end of the old thread along the area to be stitched, as shown in diagram 3, creating more padding.

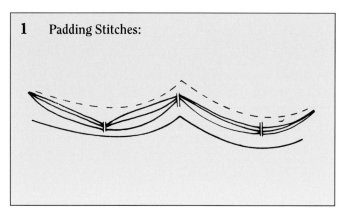

1   Padding Stitches:

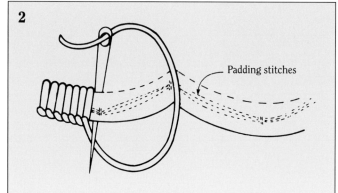

2

Padding stitches

With the new thread, tie in with short running stitches toward the already worked *caseado,* as seen in diagram 4, and bring the needle up under the last loop formed. The loose tail will be covered by the next stitches.

To tie off, the thread must be at the bottom of the stitch. Take the thread over the loop and to the back of the work. Take a nip of fabric behind the stitching and knot the thread as in a loop knot, pulling firmly. Clip the thread close to the knot.

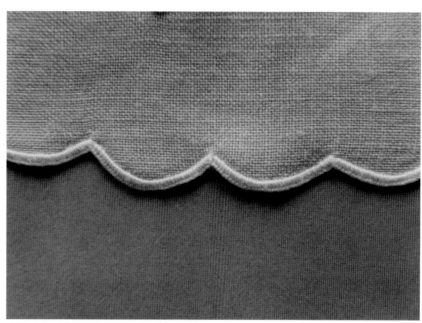

Caseado liso used on a tablecloth edge

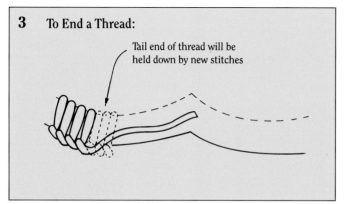

3   To End a Thread:

Tail end of thread will be held down by new stitches

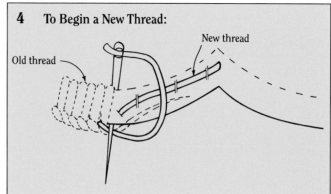

4   To Begin a New Thread:

New thread

Old thread

Cutwork with Bars

Richelieu

Although true *Richelieu* requires picots on the bars of cutwork, in Madeira all cutwork is referred to as *Richelieu*. Picots are no longer used in Madeira, because they are not cost-effective.

The padding is worked in a serpentine fashion, as shown in diagrams 1 and 2.

Remembering that the purl edge of the *caseado* (closed blanket-buttonhole) should always face the edge to be cut, tie in the thread and start the *caseado* as shown in diagram 3.

Details of a cutwork napkin corner

Work all around the top, past the bars, and around to the bottom edge. When the bars are reached, add a third leg, hooking into the purl at the top, and work *caseado* down the length of the bar as shown in diagrams 4 and 5. Continue to the next bar and repeat. The purl edge of the bars should all face the same direction.

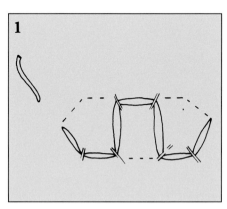

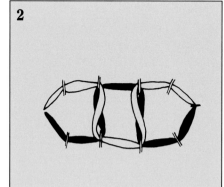

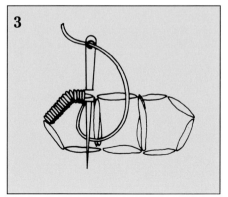

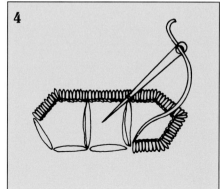

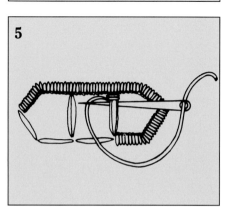

Broderie Anglaise with Bars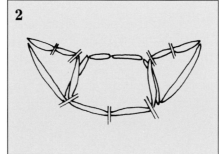

Oficial

Although this is a standard broderie anglaise technique, the Madeirans do not consider it *oficial* unless it utilizes the thread leg (bar) or *"canolinha."*

The design should be padded with long stitches in a serpentine manner. The bars are laid as a part of the padding. Thus, when padding is completed, each bar will consist of two threads, as shown in diagrams 1 and 2.

Start a tight wrap through the fabric across the upper edge, ignoring the bars. As the bars are reached on the bottom edge, lay one more thread leg across, hooking into the previously worked wraps. Take the needle between the bar threads and the ground fabric, and tightly wrap the bar threads without piercing the fabric beneath. When the end of the bar is reached, continue wrapping the outline as before and stitch on to the next bar. This is illustrated in diagram 3.

A design worked completely in *oficial* produces a smaller outline than *caseado,* but it is not as strong. Great care must be taken when cutting away the ground fabric under the bars.

Oficial used to delineate the centers of leaves

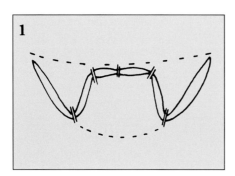

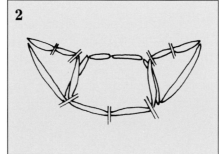

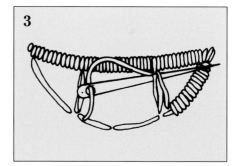

Scalloped Blanket-Buttonhole

Caseado Bastido

Caseado bastido utilizes the closed blanket-buttonhole stitch. Note that the symbol for *caseado bastido* has a smooth top line, while the bottom is more scalloped. *Bastido* means full, and the stitches are graduated and must be placed very closely together. The purl edge (base) will always face the edge to be cut. The stitch must begin at the base; otherwise, a detached chain stitch will result.

The padding stitches for *caseado bastido* consist of a zigzag running stitch with the thread doubled in the needle, as seen in diagram 1. A ¹⁄₁₆" tail is left at the top of a scallop and the padding conforms to the tiny scallops at the base, again catching two or three threads between stitches. The beginning and ending tails are left loose. Do not pull too tightly, as the fabric will pucker.

Tie in with a backstitch at the purl edge (base) and follow diagram 2, graduating the length of the stitch as the scallop deepens.

To end a thread and begin a new thread, refer to the instructions for *caseado liso* (closed blanket-buttonhole) on page 62.

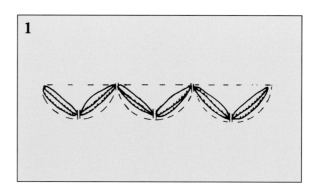

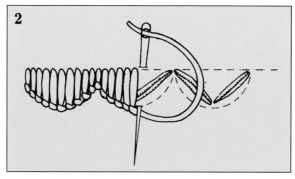

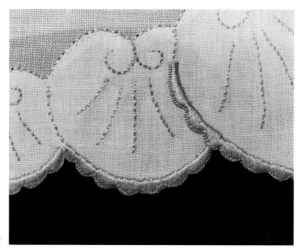

Shell-like effect of a ***caseado bastido*** *edge*

Applied Techniques

Appliqué

Although the stitches diagrammed in the previous chapter are effective when used alone, it is the combinations of fabrics and stitches that make the marvelous Madeiran embroideries unique. The techniques to be explored on the following pages are those used by generations of master artisans, dictated by the designer's conceptions and stitcher's perspective.

When Charlie Rolland brought back the technique of appliqué to Madeira, it seemed to become exclusively Madeiran. Because of Charlie's synergistic use of fabrics, color, and techniques, the art of appliqué was reborn.

Appliqué is a derivative of the French verb "appliquer" meaning "to apply." Thus, appliqué is the joining of two separate pieces of fabric. In some designs, the fabric is folded back on itself to create a second layer. When this occurs, it is called repliqué rather than appliqué.

Left: *A graceful fawn among the flora*
Right: *The delicate balance of this large motif is created with areas of **pesponto** in the heart of the **bastido**-edged petals*

Repliqué Hem

The finest repliqué hems are turned to the reverse side of the fabric and secured from there with *ponto francês* (pin stitch). The first step in creating a repliqué hem is to miter the corners. A smooth miter is effected by notching, as shown in diagram 1. Tiny running stitches are taken between A and B, allowing a ⅛" seam. The hem is turned back along the fold line to the reverse side. The raw edge is snipped and folded before stitching.

In order to make a curved edge lie flat, it is necessary to snip the fabric at intervals as illustrated in diagram 2. A concave

Fold, matching A's and stitch from A to B

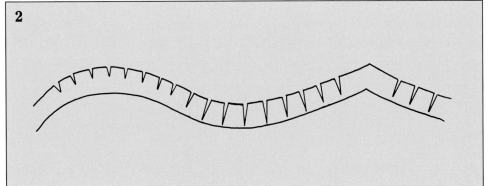

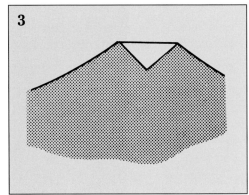

curve (⌣) is snipped almost to the drawn line. This eases the fabric, creating a smooth curve. A convex curve (⌢) is snipped midway to the design line; this prevents the turned-under edge of the fabric from pleating, which would produce peaks. To prevent the snipped edges from raveling, only a small amount is worked at a time.

The hem is stitched in a counterclockwise direction, with the hem at the top. When a sharp peak occurs in the design, the point is first folded down as shown in diagram 3, and then the sides are folded toward each other to accentuate the point, illustrated in diagrams 4 and 5. For a more finished look, only one or two threads of the fold are caught on the vertical leg of *ponto francês*. When a corner is reached, a sharper turn is achieved by taking a second vertical stitch, pulling tightly.

Napkin corner showing a repliqué hem

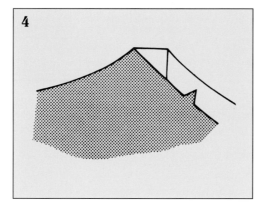

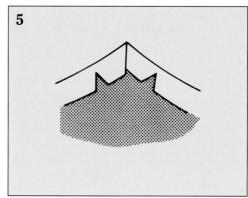

Appliqué Hem

An appliqué hem is constructed of two pieces of fabric seamed together along the outer edges. This is most often seen with contrasting colors or different weights of fabric. A linen hem appliquéd to organdy is not only exquisite, but adds stability to such a fragile fabric. When the hem is applied, the thread color should match the color of the appliqué (i.e., if a white organdy place mat is to have a blue linen border, matching blue thread would be used for *ponto francês* [pin stitch]). Either *floche* or #80 cotton thread is used. *Floche* creates a defined outline; #80 cotton thread a nearly invisible line. The snipping, folding, and stitching of an appliqué hem follow the same steps as those outlined under Repliqué Hem.

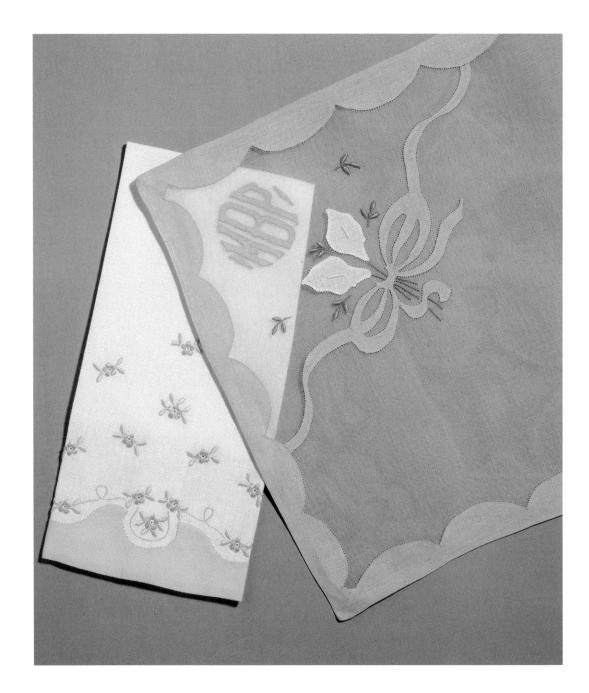

Two examples of appliqué hems

A collection of designs typical of Madeira embroidery

Appliqué Motifs

The appliquéing of motifs is a way of introducing large solid areas of color as well as dimension to a design (e.g., overlapping petals on a flower). It is also a means of creating shading in a single motif by using two colors or weights of fabric, as in a leaf—half linen and half organdy.

Definition is achieved by the addition of embroidery stitches, worked after the motif is pin stitched to the ground fabric.

The motif, whole or in parts, is stamped on the fabric, ensuring that the direction of the grain of the appliqué and the direction of the ground fabrics are the same. The pieces are cut out using a ⅛" fold allowance. Curves are clipped as previously described, design lines matched, and with the appliqué held firmly in place with the thumb and forefinger, the raw edge is turned under with the point of the needle and pin stitched down, with the work being rotated as the stitching progresses. Only extremely large or elongated pieces are basted in position.

Top: *Native Madeiran hibiscus brought to table in linen and organdy*
Bottom: *Central motif of a dresser scarf*

Left: *Place mat of linen and organdy appliqués on an organdy ground reminiscent of the art nouveau period*

Appliqué Insert

If a strong focal point is desired, an appliqué insert (always of sheer fabric) is used. The outline of the insert is transferred to both ground and insert fabrics, and the design is stitched on the fabric to be inserted. The center of the insert shape on the ground fabric is cut away to within a scant ⅛" of the insert design line. Edges are snipped and folded to the wrong side as in a repliqué hem. The insert is placed behind the opening and pin stitched in place. The raw edges of the turned-under ground fabric are trimmed to ¹⁄₁₆"; the insert edges are trimmed to ⅛", folded around the ground fabric edges, and whipped down with *ponto gant,* illustrated in the diagram below.

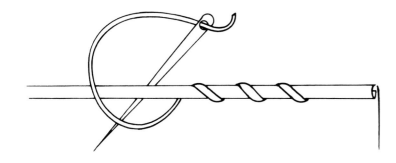

Detail of appliqué insert. Ground fabric is linen with organdy insert. The flowers are worked in ponto de sombra *(shadow work), and the ferns in* ponto de corda *(outline)*

Dimension and Shading

As mentioned earlier, shading and dimension are integral elements of appliqué. The flare of a petal or the curve of a leaf is emphasized by the use of contrasting weights, as well as by differing shades of fabric, as shown in the plume cocktail napkin at right.

The Romance Series (see pages 16-21) is the perfect example of this premise. Because the figures are in linen and the background is in organdy, they appear to be in bold relief. The detail of these figures is interpreted with various embroidery stitches. The outline-stitched hexagon pattern on the organdy ground creates the illusion of needle lace.

The petal florets of a hydrangea might be executed by using linen for two petals, and organdy for the remaining two. A flower appliquéd in one piece might have its petals defined and shaded with the use of *ponto de corda* (outline), *pesponto*

(seed stitch), or *bastido* (padded satin). The flower centers might make use of *granitos* (rondels), *Richelieu* (cutwork with bars), or *ilhó aberto* (open eyelet).

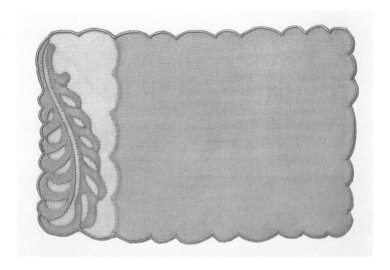

Bottom: *Granitos and granitos bastido used in profusion to define and enhance the designs*

The highest degree of dimension is achieved with detached appliqué. A butterfly worked in this fashion will appear to be fluttering. The fine detail of the butterfly wings are embroidered, the outside edge of the wings worked in *caseado liso* (closed blanket-buttonhole), and the whole cut away. The body of the butterfly is created by working through two layers of fabric in *bastido* (padded satin), effectively attaching the motif to the base fabric. Antennae are then stitched on the ground fabric, as seen in the photograph at right.

*The unfurling petals of this stylized peony design are created with **bastido***

Right: *Close-up of appliqué butterfly*
Below: *The epitome of detached appliqué*

The Projects

Fingertip towel

Calla lily table mat

Cocktail napkin

This section features five embroidery projects from the design collection of Herman Klein. They are included so that you may incorporate the stitches and applied techniques described previously in Chapters 4 and 5, respectively. These particular pieces have been chosen because they are simple, yet elegant examples of Madeira embroidery and will serve as lovely additions to any home or embroidery collection.

Ascot

Place mat

The projects pictured here are from the archives of Imperial Linens and have been reproduced with their gracious permission.

General Information

All of the projects shown on the following pages were stitched with *floche*. Linen and organdy were the fabrics used to create these projects. For individual stitches, refer to the stitch section. Instructions for hems and appliqués will be found in the section on applied techniques.

To transfer a design, allow a 2" fabric margin on all sides past the design. Trace the design on a separate piece of paper. Place the design behind the fabric and trace the design on the fabric with a washable cloth pencil or pen.

When working a *caseado* (closed blanket-buttonhole) or *oficial* (broderie anglaise with bars) edge, do not cut away the excess fabric until the border has been completely finished and the piece washed.

Cocktail Napkin

1. Turn back the border for a repliqué hem and attach with *ponto francês* (pin stitch).

2. Stitch the *viuva* (widow) flowers, shading from dark (inner corner) and radiating from medium to light.

3. Work the *granitos* (rondels); these may also be shaded.

4. Stitch the leaves using *fôlha fechada* (satin leaf).

5. Work the tendrils in *ponto de corda* (outline).

Fabric Requirements:

8-½" × 11" green linen

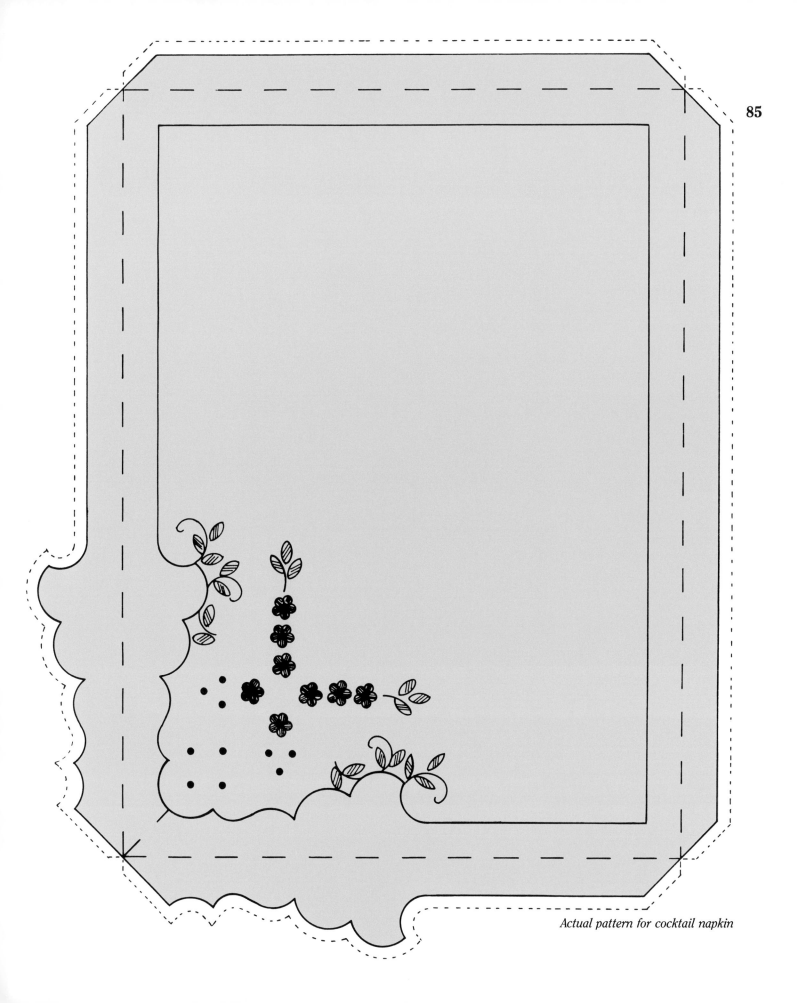

Actual pattern for cocktail napkin

Calla Lily Table Mat

1. Work the *caseado liso* (closed blanket-buttonhole) edge.

2. Appliqué the calla lily and the bud with *ponto francês* (pin stitch).

3. Attach the linen half of the leaves to the organdy side with *ponto francês,* then appliqué the whole leaf to the ground fabric. Stitch the veins in *ponto de corda* (outline).

4. Form the calyx at the base of the flower with *bastido* (padded satin). Use this stitch to fashion the small leaves at the lower left of the design as well.

5. Work the stamen (in the center of the calla lily) in heavy *bastido.*

6. Define the curves of the flower and the stems with *ponto de corda.*

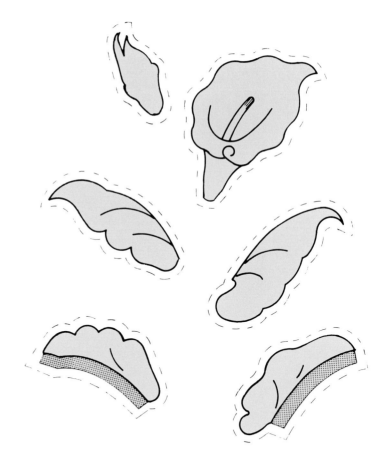

Calla lily appliqués

Fabric Requirements:

10" square blue linen
3" square white linen
3" square green linen
3" square pale green organdy

Exact size of table mat

Fingertip Towel

1. Work *caseado liso* (closed blanket-buttonhole) edge.

2. Attach the flower and bud appliqués with *ponto francês* (pin stitch).

3. Attach the leaf appliqués with *ponto francês*.

4. Work the bases of the stems in *chão* (satin stitch), continuing the stems with *ponto de corda* (outline).

5. Work the two small furled leaves in *chão*.

6. Define the curl of the petals and the veins of the leaves with *ponto atraz* (backstitch).

7. Use *ponto de corda* for the stamens and pistils with *granitos bastido* (rondels) radiating from the center.

Fabric Requirements:

14" × 21" white linen
5" square coral linen
4" × 5" green linen

Finished size: 12³/₄ × 19"

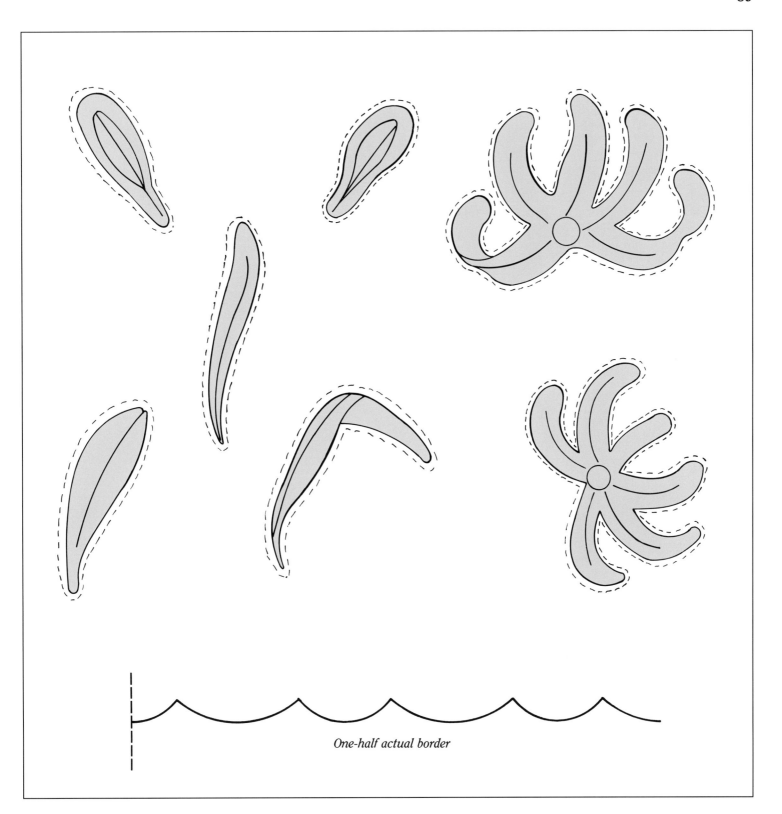

One-half actual border

Ascot

1. Machine stay stitch the length, allowing ½" fabric on each side, to be finished as a ¼" turned hem.

2. Stitch the ends of the ascot in *oficial* (broderie anglaise with bars); work the inverted teardrop shapes incorporated into the border with *bastido* (padded satin).

3. Pad the swan, then pad the pentagon frame around the swan, laying and wrapping the bars as the padding progresses.

4. Work the body of the swan in *oficial* in the following order:

    Inner arch of the neck beneath the beak.

    Around the beak and head to the first section of the wing.

    Below the beak, around the breast and lower body, to the bottom section of the wing.

    The lower wing section.

    The remaining neck section and then the upper wing area.

5. Use a *granitos* (rondel) for the eye.

6. Define the brow with very small *ponto de cordão* (whipped running stitch).

7. Form the spiraling tendrils in *ponto de cordão,* then work the teardrops in *bastido.*

8. Create the three small circles on each side of the design with *ilhó fechado* (satin circle).

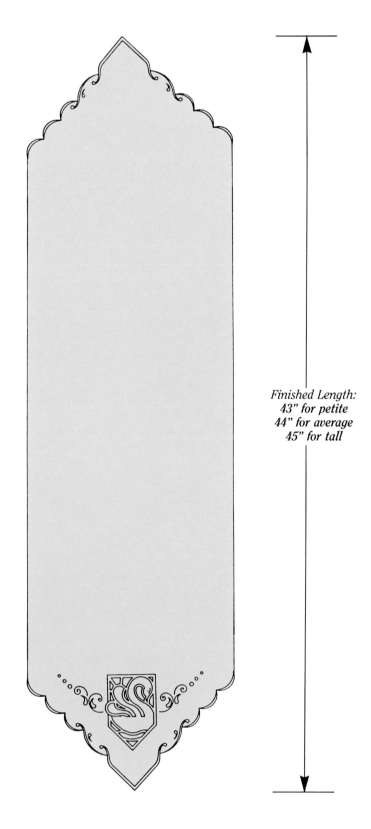

Finished Length:
43" for petite
44" for average
45" for tall

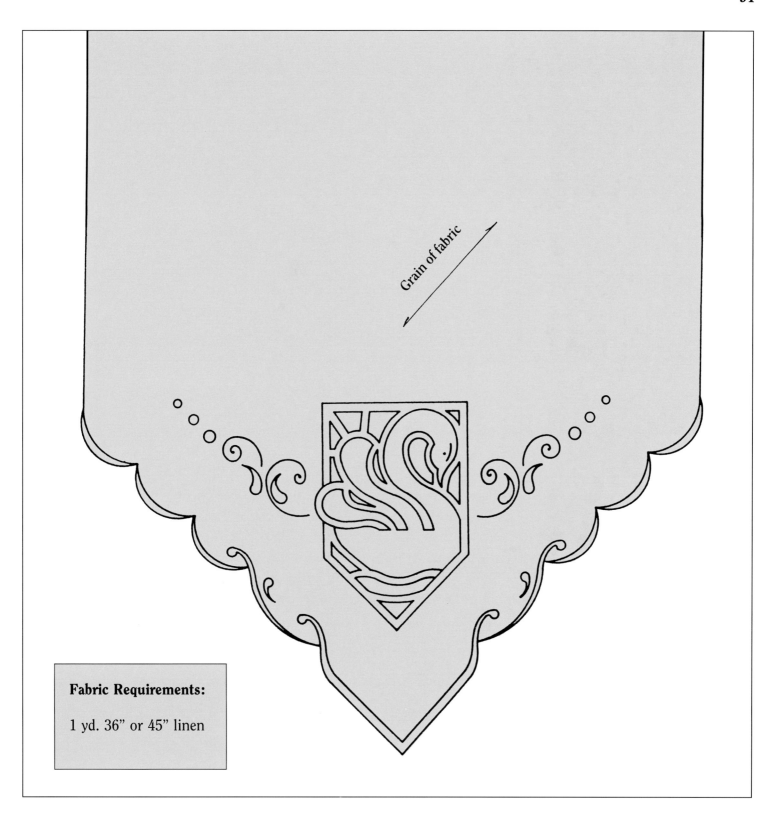

Grain of fabric

Fabric Requirements:

1 yd. 36" or 45" linen

Place Mat

1. Apply the linen ground to the organdy border with *ponto francês* (pin stitch). On the wrong side, whip the raw edges under with *ponto gant* (see Appliqué Insert on page 77).

2. Work the edge of the mat in alternating scallops of *caseado liso* (closed blanket-buttonhole) and *caseado bastido* (scalloped blanket-buttonhole).

3. Appliqué the leaves to the organdy border; define the veins in *ponto atraz* (backstitch).

4. Stitch the stems and tendrils in *ponto de corda* (outline).

5. Form the small flowers with *granitos* (rondels) in the *viuva* (widow) pattern; use single *granitos* for the small buds.

6. Use *fôlha fechada* (satin leaf) for the leaves.

Note: A matching napkin may be made of any size using a plain corner of the mat as a guide. Sprinkle *viuva* flowers at random around the edges and finish with a repliqué hem.

Match up to dotted line on opposite page

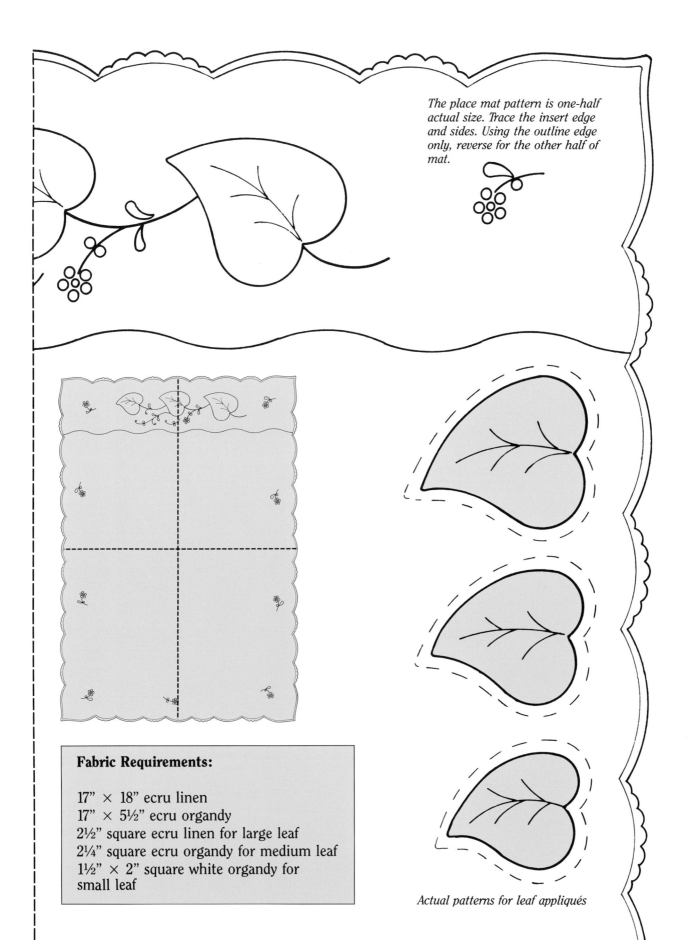

The place mat pattern is one-half actual size. Trace the insert edge and sides. Using the outline edge only, reverse for the other half of mat.

Fabric Requirements:

17" × 18" ecru linen
17" × 5½" ecru organdy
2½" square ecru linen for large leaf
2¼" square ecru organdy for medium leaf
1½" × 2" square white organdy for small leaf

Actual patterns for leaf appliqués

Supply Directory

Fibers:

	United States	Britain
Floche	Needlefantasies P.O. Box 7749 Dallas, TX 75209	Coats Marketing Division 39 Durham Street Glasgow G41 1BS
Stranded cotton	City Stitcher 46 E. Chicago Ave. Chicago, Il 60611	Dunlicraft Ltd (DMC UK Distributors) Pullman Road Wigston Leicester LE8 2DY
#80 Cotton thread	Lacis 2945 Adeline Street Berkeley, CA 94703	Gutermann-Perivale Wadsworth Road Greenford Middlesex UB6 7JS

Fabrics:

Linen and batiste	Margaret Pierce Inc. 1816 Pembroke Rd. Greensboro, NC 27408	MacCulloch & Wallis 15-16 Dering Street London W1R OBH
Pastel organdy and chiffon	Jerry Brown Imported Fabrics 37 W. 57th Street New York, NY 10019	Borovicks Fabrics Ltd 16 Berwick Street London W1

Embroidery Tools:

#7 Between needles and finger shields	Needlefantasies P.O. Box 7749 Dallas, TX 75209	The Nimble Thimble 26 The Green Bilton Rugby Warwickshire

Embroidered Linens:

	Imperial Linens Inc. 302 Fifth Ave. New York, NY 10001	

Index

English

Portuguese

Credits

Production Notes

Production Supervisor:	Doris Laurence
Designers:	Loraine Machlin, Clark Kellogg
Illustrations:	Cindy Garcia
Type:	Clearface
Stock:	80# Patina Coated Matte

Printed and bound by Heritage Press

Photography Credits

Courtesy of the Kulla Family	(pp. 12,13,14)
Courtesy of Imperial Linens	(pp. 12,14-23,31,43)
Ulf Skogsbergh	(pp. 3,6,9,25,35,36,41, 53,61,64,67-82)
Robert Whiteside	(pp. 33,83)
Carolyn Walker and Kathy Holman	(pp. 7,26-30,32,44-52, 54-60,63,66)